MAKING CARS AT
COWLEY

MAKING CARS AT
COWLEY
FROM MORRIS TO MINI

GILLIAN BARDSLEY AND
STEPHEN LAING

BRITISH MOTOR INDUSTRY HERITAGE TRUST

First published 2006
This new edition published 2013

The History Press
The Mill, Brimscombe Port
Stroud, Gloucestershire, GL5 2QG
www.thehistorypress.co.uk

British Library Cataloguing in Publication Data.
A catalogue record for this book is available from the British Library.

ISBN 978 0 7524 9146 2

Typesetting and origination by The History Press
Printed in Great Britain

Contents

Acknowledgements

Thanks to John Bacchus and Oliver White for their generous and knowledgeable assistance with picture research and proofreading for the original edition. Likewise Colin Corke for extensive help in preparing the second, revised version. Also Malcolm Boyns, Lisa Stevens and Steph Sykes for much time spent sourcing and scanning images.

Those interested in the life of William Morris, Lord Nuffield can learn much about this pioneer of the motor industry by visiting the reconstruction of his office in the Heritage Motor Centre at Gaydon near Warwick and then paying a visit to his home at Nuffield Place near Henley-on-Thames in Oxfordshire.

Picture Credits

Most of the photographic material in this book is taken from the comprehensive archive collections of the British Motor Industry Heritage Trust. Additional photographs were provided by Mr Harry Turley (155 bottom) who has made a photographic record of the redevelopment of the Cowley site, and BMIHT Archivist Gillian Bardsley (13 bottom, 16 bottom, 158 bottom).

One
The Changing Face
of Cowley

In 1913 an ambitious young businessman named William Morris converted a derelict Military College on the outskirts of Oxford into an assembly hall for motor vehicles. He thus opened the first chapter in one of the most extraordinary success stories of the British motor industry, becoming Lord Nuffield and a multi-millionaire in the process. From Morris Motors and Pressed Steel, via the British Motor Corporation and British Leyland to its role as part of BMW, car manufacture at Cowley has been a significant player. Though the old factory chimneys have given way to more modern developments, Oxford today would be a very different place without its influence.

Part of the Cowley complex in 1972, featuring the body conveyor over the Oxford Eastern bypass, newly improved for Morris Marina production.

1919 saw the first phase of factory expansion when foundations for a new body shop were laid on the site of allotments opposite the former Military College, a building which now carried the words 'Morris Oxford Cars'.

By 1921 an aerial view showed the original three-storey buildings of the Military College surrounded by lower, purpose-built structures with distinctive zig-zag roofs, which more than doubled the size of the Morris Motors factory.

The North Works in 1925. The pile of building materials behind the Morris Cowley 'Bullnose' tourer indicates that the expansion process was continuing apace.

This steady progress was halted by the Second World War. In 1944 the Morris Commercial lorry leaving the factory gate was fitted with headlamp masks to comply with blackout regulations.

Cowley in 1966. By this date, at the end of the BMC era, the site had reached its largest extent. On the left was the railway station and distribution area, which was as important to communications as the road network. With Pressed Steel in the foreground, the Oxford Eastern bypass ran from left to right across the middle of the picture, bridged by the bodyshell conveyor.

Two distinctive chimneys stood at the centre of the factory complex surrounded by the extensive slatted roofs of North Works (right), South Works (left) and Pressed Steel (bottom). Garsington Road ran from bottom left to top right in the direction of Oxford until it met Hollow Way at the top of the picture. On this corner was the Nuffield Press building (formerly the Military College).

This was a typical Oxford scene in 1928 (with Morris products well represented). Evidence of the growing motor industry could easily be found on the streets of the city.

In this tranquil scene of 1949 the photographer has discovered a solitary Morris Minor sitting in the heart of the university district surrounded by student cycles on a street otherwise empty of vehicles.

The Morris Cowley station on the Great Western Railway was built specifically to serve the factory, delivering both goods and workers. In 1954 a Morris Minor on trade plates approached the bridge to climb the hill which would take it back to the factory. On the way it passed a hoarding proclaiming the numerous marques of the Nuffield Organisation.

On the other side of the bridge in 2006 it was two BMW MINIs which carried trade plates as they mingled with the traffic, having possibly just completed the same journey.

The many faces of William Morris, Lord Nuffield: *top*; confident motor manufacturer, *bottom*; nervous peer of the realm and relaxed businessman ...

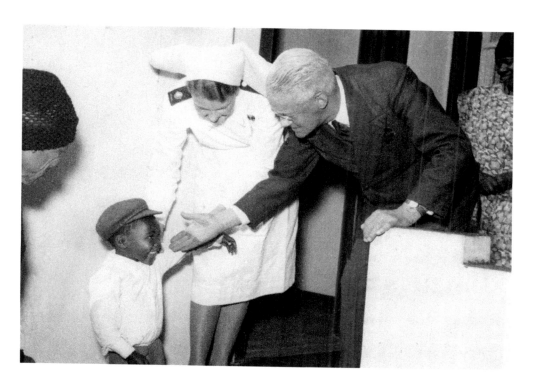

... *top*; compassionate philanthropist, *bottom*; enthusiastic international traveller and playful dog lover.

1992 – 'Gate 10' on Garsington Road in the shadow of one of the distinctive factory chimneys. This was one of the entrance points to the old Morris Motors complex which was to be demolished the following year.

By 2006 North and South Works had been replaced by a modern business park. Not far from where the chimneys had once pointed into the sky, the only remaining clue to the historical significance of the site is an obelisk, known as the 'Nuffield Needle'. Embossed at its base is a Morris ox, modelled after the bonnet badge of a Morris Minor 1000.

Two
William Morris:
Making a Start

William Morris began as a humble cycle maker but by 1913 he had realised his dream to assemble a car. He secured an order for 400 vehicles and delivered the first one personally.

William Morris in his first Morris Oxford 'Bullnose' outside Stewart & Ardern's London showroom.

William Richard Morris was born in Worcestershire on 10 October 1877. His father, Frederick, was a farm bailiff, but he and his wife Emily suffered from poor health. When their family began to grow, they decided to move back to their original home of Oxford. William's ambition was to be a doctor, but as the only surviving son of an invalid father he left school at fourteen to support the family. In 1892 he set up his own cycle business with the grand sum of £4 capital. Using the back of his parents' home as a workshop, he turned the front rooms into his showroom.

The business prospered and in 1901 he moved to a shop in Oxford's High Street. He formed a partnership with fellow cyclist Joseph Cooper to provide capital for expansion into motorcycles and they took on some disused livery stables at Longwall for repair work but Cooper soon dropped out, uneasy at the level of risk involved in the investment. He and Morris remained friends for, as the latter would later say, 'he could have been where I am now if things had been different'. In 1904 Morris formed another partnership to set up the Oxford Automobile and Cycle Agency which drew him into the motor car repair and sales business. His partners proved unreliable and Morris was reduced to standing in the rain bidding for his own tools. He vowed that he would keep control of his own affairs from then on.

So he concentrated his effort on the 'Oxford Garage' at Longwall, which he had begun with Cooper, and it quickly gained a reputation for quality of service. In 1910 new premises were constructed on the same site and officially named 'The Morris Garage'. It was here, in 1912, that he fulfilled his ambition to build his own car. The first British motor car factory had been set up in Coventry in 1896 so Morris was a relative latecomer. Existing firms took great pride in manufacturing every part of the vehicle themselves but Morris realised that he could produce an automobile more cheaply by sourcing components from individual suppliers. His first car was a two-seater 8.9hp tourer advertised at a price of £175. It was designed with reliability and low running costs in mind and named the 'Morris Oxford', acquiring the nickname 'Bullnose' from the distinctive shape of its radiator. A new company called WRM Motors, based on the initials of his name, was set up to market it.

Morris had secured an order from London motor agents Stewart & Ardern for 400 cars, which meant he needed larger premises and a disused military college in Temple Cowley provided the solution. In 1915 a four-seater 1.5 litre 'Morris Cowley' joined the Morris Oxford as part of his product range. Few of these were made, however, before the demands of the First World War overshadowed civilian motor manufacture. Initially, Morris feared for his fledgling company. Because his business was based on assembly rather than engineering, his funds were tied up in stock which was useless as long as the war lasted. Profit turned to loss.

He turned his energy to improving methods of munitions manufacture to keep his company solvent. In 1916, he secured a contract to produce mine sinkers, offering to increase production from 40 to 250 per week. By employing his methods of sub-contracting individual component manufacture and concentrating on assembly, Morris reached a peak output of 2,000 units per week. Profits returned to Cowley and Morris earned an OBE for his efforts.

As a young man, William Morris (left) loved cycling. He was a member of a local bicycle club, which is where he met his future wife, Elizabeth Anstey. As a keen racing competitor he also won many medals and trophies.

William Morris and his family in 1896. He is standing with his sister Alice; his mother Emily, father Frederick and sister Emily are sitting in front. Four younger siblings had all died as infants and his parents were also in poor health, relying on William to provide for the family.

After leaving school at the age of fourteen, he chose to set up his own business, building and repairing bicycles from the family home in James Street, Oxford. The business prospered, enabling him to move to this shop in the High Street in 1901, where he branched out into motorcycles.

In 1903 he went into business with two partners to create the 'Oxford Automobile and Cycle Agency'. The staff posed for a photograph, with Morris sitting at the centre, but the business failed after barely a year. Morris went back to working on his own account.

In 1909 Morris opened a small additional workshop in St Cross Road where he overhauled and repaired motorcycles, which were becoming increasingly popular and were often fitted with sidecars like the one on the right to increase their usefulness.

His main trading base was the 'Oxford Garage' at Longwall where he operated his core business of cycle manufacture and repair. The original buildings, shown here in 1907, were converted from an extensive livery stables in Holywell Street, Oxford, backing onto the city walls.

He began to garage and maintain the cars of Oxford undergraduates. This led him to acquire his own fleet of cars which he hired out complete with driver. In this picture he is in the passenger seat of the car on the extreme right.

By 1910 the 'Oxford Garage' had become the 'Morris Garage' and the building had been rebuilt with a modern frontage. His current fleet of hire cars was parked outside.

Morris did not intend to stop at motorcycles and car hire. It was at Longwall that he built his first car, the Morris Oxford. Front left is Joseph Cooper, with whom he remained friends despite the failure of their business partnership.

WAKING UP OLD OXFORD.

THE MODERN St. GEORGE AND THE DRAGON.

MORRIS DANCING AT OXFORD.

Morris was becoming an important figure in Oxford. He was frequently caricatured as a threat to established interests, 'Waking Up Old Oxford' (left). When he was denied a licence to compete with tram operators, he set up a fleet of six Daimler buses which became so popular that the City Council was forced to back down. The councillors (right) were depicted angrily 'Morris dancing' to his tune.

Once Morris had obtained a substantial order for his cars, he acquired the old Military College in Hollow Way to launch his career as a motor manufacturer. In 1913 one week's production of the Morris Oxford 'Bullnose' was lined up outside in the afternoon sun.

The Morris-Oxford Light Car.

1914   **1914**

Manufacturers: **W.R.M. MOTORS, LTD.,**

Codes: *A1 A.B.C. (4th & 5th)*
Engineering (2nd edition) Liebers, Western Union.

Telegrams and Cables:
" *VOITURETTE, COWLEY—OXON.*"

Telephone: **590** *Oxford.*

THE COWLEY MOTOR WORKS,
COWLEY, - near OXFORD.

Wholesale and Shipping Agent:
W. H. M. BURGESS,
40 GLASSHOUSE STREET, LONDON, W.

The front cover from an early brochure for the 'Morris-Oxford Light Car'. Morris named his new business 'W.R.M. Motors' after the initials of his name and adopted the ox as his symbol.

He had hardly begun when the business was interrupted by the outbreak of the First World War in 1914. Morris obtained an order for mine sinkers and increased production by applying more efficient methods of assembly. This train was loaded with sinkers ready for despatch in 1917.

As the war progressed, most of the factory was given over to armaments and demand for cars ebbed away. This view from 1917 shows equipment and components for munitions assembly.

A 1918 victory parade featured a fleet of 'Trench Warfare' trucks decorated with the Union Flag and loaded with the mine sinkers he had produced so successfully. Among the drivers were some of the 400 women who had been engaged for war work after compulsory male conscription to the army was introduced in 1915.

Peace returned and factory workers respectfully listened to the factory band during Armistice Day celebrations.

By 1919, the paraphernalia of war production had been cleared away. This view in August of that year showed that civilian vehicles were once again being made in earnest.

Three
The Move to Mass Production

During the 1920s and '30s William Morris became Lord Nuffield and Morris Motors grew into the Nuffield Organisation, becoming a major player in the British motor industry alongside the Austin Motor Company. The theme of these years was the constant improvement in production methods, and Leonard Lord was chosen to orchestrate the final transition to mass production.

In 1936 Leonard Lord and Lord Nuffield handed over the 100,000th Morris Eight to Mr Alfred Allen, whose job was assistant organiser for the Allotment Gardens for the Unemployed.

In 1919 the company was renamed Morris Motors but the interruption of war meant that as yet only around 1,500 cars had been produced. Pre-war manufacture had been constrained by the three-storey layout of the Military College which required parts and sub-assemblies to be moved between floors for different stages of assembly. The first step to address this problem had been taken in 1914 by erecting a steel structure in the centre courtyard on what was once the military parade ground. When production restarted in 1919, this area was used to create a flow system. Chassis were wheeled on 'slave' wheels along tracks from station to station where each component was then fitted. So the stations became fixed, with the cars rather than the workers moving between them. The stocks of parts that had counted against Cowley before the war meant production could restart almost immediately once peace was declared. These factors allowed Morris to catch up quickly with more established manufacturers such as Austin and Ford who had also been stalled by the need to produce munitions.

As 1921 approached Cowley faced another hurdle, an unexpected slump in the world economy. The factory's output dropped from over 250 per week in September 1920 to 74 per week the following January. Morris used the goodwill of his suppliers to get parts in advance of payment on the understanding that he would find a way to sell his cars. He also negotiated a reduction in the margin which his distributors got from their sales. Finally he made the bravest move of all. He cut his prices by up to 25 per cent. The result was almost immediate. Ahead of its rivals, Morris Motors' sales rose, regaining their previous level.

Manufacture began to move away from the outdated Military College when construction of new buildings began on allotments across the road. In 1921 the complex which would become known as 'North Works' was underway and by 1926 'B' to 'K' blocks had been completed, covering more than 40 acres. 'P' block was completed in 1929, bringing the size of the factory to over 80 acres. South Works was begun in 1937 to accommodate wartime production.

His business success and his philanthropy earned William Morris a knighthood in 1929. Later he was elevated to the peerage, becoming a Baron in 1934 and a Viscount in 1938. He took the title of Lord Nuffield from a local Oxfordshire village. His expanding group of factories, stretching from Oxford to Coventry and Birmingham, became known as the Nuffield Organisation. But he could not afford to fall behind as competitors adopted ever more advanced production methods. He chose Leonard Lord, who had made a great success out of running subsidiary Morris Engines, for the task of reorganising Cowley's production areas and the move to full mass production began in earnest. The chassis were now constructed on a moving assembly line while overhead cranes and conveyors delivered components and sub-assemblies to the correct place on the track.

It was both a professional and personal disappointment to Lord Nuffield when a disgruntled Leonard Lord left in 1936 and later joined his major rival, the Austin Motor Company. But Morris Motors continued to prosper, recording its one millionth car in May 1939, the first British motor company to reach this landmark, some seven years ahead of Austin, thanks to the intervention of a Second World War when civilian production was once again suspended for the duration.

In 1919 Morris renamed his company 'Morris Motors' and began to build up his manufacturing business once again. This was a typical view of a period machine shop, with its hand-operated equipment including a myriad of unprotected overhead belts and pulleys.

Though women were less prominent in the factory after the war, they were still engaged on tasks such as small component assembly, as in this view where they were gauging axle components.

During the 1920s the layout of the factory was constantly improved to create a production flow but most tasks were still labour-intensive. Installing the engine, for example, required a simple pulley, four men in flat caps and, on the left, a supervisor in a suit.

Simple techniques were increasingly being applied to maximise production. In the 'C' block paint shop, assembled chassis were manoeuvred from the track onto turntables so they could be more easily manipulated into one of four paint spray booths.

Once in the booth, the chassis was held in a cradle and rotated, making each part accessible and enabling two men to spray it in just a few minutes. Health and safety was not a major consideration, the dress code consisting of a starched collar and tie underneath the workwear, along with a flat cap.

Once painted, the chassis were moved through drying kilns, pulled along by a system of chains and ratchets. When they emerged the steering wheels, which can be seen hanging at the end of the kilns, were attached.

Installation of certain chassis components required extra height. At the relevant stations, cars could be lifted by hydraulic jacks and then dropped back onto the line to proceed to the next area. Note the wooden block to get that extra bit of height to suit the assembler.

The pneumatic tyres were fitted to wheel rims in a dedicated area separate from the rest of the chassis. Once again this was a labour-intensive process, involving dozens of men to fit the tyres and wheels together, ready to be bolted onto the completed cars.

For the journey along the track, the cars were fitted with 'slave' or disc wheels to move them along. These were replaced with the correct wheels further down the assembly line.

In the mounting department in 1930, these Morris Oxfords were being trimmed and finished after receiving their bodies. The sign above outlines the work being carried out: fitting of the rear screen, bonnet, ventilator and lino to foot and bottom board and attaching the bonnet beading.

The Subscription List will close on or before the 14th day of July, 1926.

MORRIS MOTORS (1926) LIMITED

(Incorporated under the Companies Acts, 1908 to 1917.)

AUTHORISED CAPITAL:

3,000,000	Seven and a-Half per Cent. Cumulative Preference Shares of £1 each	-	-	-	£3,000,000
2,000,000	Ordinary Shares of £1 each	-	-	-	£2,000,000

ISSUE OF

3,000,000 Seven and a-Half per Cent. Cumulative Preference Shares of £1 each at par.

PAYABLE:—

On Application	-	-	-	2s. 6d.
On Allotment	-	-	-	7s. 6d.
On the 16th day of August, 1926	-	-	5s. 0d.
On the 16th day of September, 1926	-	-	5s. 0d.
				£1 0s. 0d.

William Morris was prospering and on 29 June 1926 he registered Morris Motors as a public company. Morris kept control by remaining the sole owner of ordinary shares but an issue of preference shares provided new finance which enabled him to begin the process of buying up first his own suppliers, and then rival firms such as Wolseley and Riley.

A sign of his success was a visit from HRH the Prince of Wales on 24 May 1927. The Prince chatted to a factory worker, former Company Sergeant Major Brooks VC. Sir William Morris, in the foreground with his hat tilted back casually, was in discussion with another of his employees.

Once the chassis was finished and the front wings attached, items such as wiring and lamps could be installed. Each worker rested his personal box of tools near his feet. The crude tracks which were used to guide the cars from station to station on their wheels are clearly visible.

Vehicles were tested on the road, often before the complete bodywork had been fitted. These chassis, heading off on trade plates in 1929, were sporty MGs rather than standard Morrises. The MG Car Company was one of Morris' personal investments and took its name from the initials of 'Morris Garages'. It was so successful that it outgrew the Edmund Road premises pictured here and moved to nearby Abingdon where production remained until 1980.

Back at Morris Motors in 1926: this car, with rather more complete bodywork, had also been fitted with trade plates and was being primed with petrol ready for a run.

On a carousel! In 1932 production techniques were still evolving. The rear axle and torque tube assembly lines were kept apart, with separate differential gear and propeller shaft lines converging on the torque tube line. Both ended in this 'start stand' which held the torque tube in place whilst the rear axle was bolted onto it. Behind them, the workmen had leaned their bicycles against the girders and partition where their hats and coats hung on hooks.

Morris was expanding overseas. In its Bombay (Mumbai) office during the 1920s a room of earnest clerks administered the business on the Indian subcontinent.

Visiting dignitaries from the colonies were often welcomed to the factory too. In 1928 a party from the African Gold Coast (modern-day Ghana) posed with Miles Thomas (fourth from right), a journalist who joined William Morris to mastermind his innovative publicity campaign.

More than 10,000 people worked for the Morris group of companies by 1930 and over half of them were employed at Cowley. When home time came it was the bicycle which was the standard method of transport for the motor car worker.

By this time, North Works covered over 80 acres. Building work continued apace, though the horse and cart was still very much a part of the building trade, even when constructing a motor car factory.

Change was on the way and Ford Motor Company's production methods in particular had become the role model throughout the motor industry. Yet when Henry Ford (centre) visited Cowley in 1928, Morris was not there to greet him, choosing instead to meet him the next day in London.

Morris (left) entrusted the modernisation of his factory to his protégé Leonard Lord (right). In 1933 they discussed their plans. Appropriately, a framed picture of a motor show display sat on the cupboard behind them, while a portrait of Morris hung on the wall to the right.

The introduction of the Morris Eight in 1934 enabled Morris Motors to remain highly competitive in the small car market. It was produced using suitably advanced methods, being pulled along the track on a pulley rather than pushed from station to station on its wheels.

Even the delivery of wheels to the track was done mechanically, eliminating the need for piles of wheels stacked next to the line.

This picture from 1938 shows how complex the assembly hall had become. The cars were built on a series of continuously moving lines.

Sub-assemblies were brought in by overhead conveyors and arrived at exactly the right spot on the line. Other components were to hand in trays which lined either side of the track.

Nor did the car have to leave the factory for the road test. Here, a Morris Eight was tested on a rolling road. The machine in the background measured the performance of the car.

Other tests were more mysterious and the facilities somewhat cruder. These intrepid workers appear to be tilting the car onto a bolster to investigate its stability.

By 1939 the Morris Eight Series E was being produced in quantity. It was one of the earliest cars to have its headlamps embedded in the wings rather than perched on top, a radical departure in contemporary styling.

Above left: Scottish entertainer Harry Lauder put his signature next to a caricature in the 1935 visitors book.

Above right: HRH the Duke of Kent (centre) also visited in 1936, but shortly afterwards Len Lord fell out with Morris, who was now Lord Nuffield, and later joined rival company Austin.

Nevertheless Morris Motors prospered and in May 1939 a landmark one millionth Morris car was reached. It was a Morris Fourteen which Lord Nuffield donated to the Ladies Association of Guy's Hospital who raffled it at their village fete to raise nearly £1,700 for their funds.

Four
The Revolution in Coachbuilding

The final step towards mass production was the arrival of the pressed steel body process. The old methods, requiring gangs of men labouring for several weeks to construct a single body, were gradually replaced by massive presses which could stamp out hundreds of identical panels with great speed and efficiency.

Setting up a hand-built ash frame on a jig in 1933.

Bodies were manufactured separately to the chassis using traditional coach-building methods. These involved building up a wooden frame, panelling it with metal, hand-painting and finishing. Skilled teams of carpenters, metal workers and upholsterers were required and the process did not lend itself to flow production. In the earliest days, the engineering elements and coachwork were combined by manhandling the finished body onto the chassis with the assistance of crude pulleys.

By the 1930s the operation of marrying body to chassis had been significantly improved. At Cowley, blocks 'G' and 'K' were specially amalgamated to accommodate this process. After being painted and trimmed, the bodies travelled from one end of the shop by overhead conveyor to the middle point of the line. The chassis came from the other direction to join them. At the point where they met, the body was lowered onto the chassis by a system of winches. But the effort required to get the bodywork ready for fitting to the chassis still depended on the labour-intensive jobs already described, thus preventing most car factories from reaping the full benefits of mass-production techniques which were being developed for the mechanical parts of the vehicle.

On a trip to North America, William Morris was introduced to Edward G. Budd of Philadelphia, who had pioneered the all-steel body which was revolutionising the North American motor industry. The whole structure of the body was built up by pressed steel panels, welded together to make a single body unit. Morris immediately recognised this was the final piece of the flow production jigsaw. With considerable foresight he invested in a joint company with the Budd Company and the bankers J. Henry Schroeder & Co. to establish the Pressed Steel Company of Great Britain in 1926.

The new works was built across the road from the Morris Motors factory and took up around 10 acres, equipped with sixty heavy steel presses which had to be manoeuvred into place before the structure of the building was completed, such was their size. Many of the men engaged to build and equip the factory came from the ship industry. The two factories together became a dominant factor in the economy and landscape of the area.

Morris was eager to see a quick return on this large investment but was initially frustrated by quality problems caused to some extent by the unfamiliarity of the workforce with the new techniques. Some of the first pressings failed from buckling, rippling and burst steel and models for 1927 which should have had all-steel bodies had to be fitted with composite coachwork. But the problems were soon solved and before too long the factory was turning out bodies efficiently and speedily.

Then the company hit another problem. The fact that William Morris had an interest in the ownership of Pressed Steel began to affect business. The new enterprise could only succeed if it received a wide range of orders, but other motor companies were reluctant to use it because of his involvement. In 1930 he therefore relinquished his shares in Pressed Steel and the company went on to flourish, making pressings for a wide variety of manufacturers including Hillman, Austin, Jaguar, Rover, Rolls-Royce and Standard. It would remain independent until 1966 when its merger with the British Motor Corporation brought it back into the same fold as its old partner, Morris Motors.

Wood was an essential material in the coach-building process, requiring a sawmill department.

Traditionally bodies were built up by hand, based on a basic wooden frame often made of ash. It was important to ensure that the bodies were accurately put together and setting up the body jig was a complicated and skilled process.

The wooden frames were covered with hand-beaten individual metal panels. These Bullnose bodies, having received their metal skin and upholstered seats, had been mounted on trestles for trimming and finishing. On the right, bodies awaiting attention were stacked on their bulkhead ends.

Complete with radiators and wheels, the Bullnoses were pushed into parallel booths where, under bright lights to detect blemishes, they received a final coat of paint.

The North Works 'B' block body shop was built in 1921-2. The long lines of men looking out from their workstations shows the high number of people required by the older methods of coach-building.

Coach-builders worked in gangs of four or five and spent many hours on difficult manual tasks such as rubbing down and final preparation of bodywork.

Elsewhere upholstered seats were stuffed with horsehair and stacked ready to be installed once the body had been fitted to the car.

Marrying body with chassis in the early 1920s was a difficult process. Here two men were manipulating the frame for a wooden van with some difficulty by hand from the ground onto the chassis beside it.

A breakthrough came with the creation of the Pressed Steel Company of Great Britain in 1926. Such was the weight and size of the steel presses that the end of the building was left open until they had been installed.

Once they were set up they quickly began to stamp out a vast number of panels and complicated shapes, like these wings, became much simpler to produce.

The new factory was constructed across the road from Morris Motors and the main buildings covered some 10 acres.

P·S·C "one-piece" bodies now adopted for the newest cars

PRESSED STEEL COMPANY
OXFORD

An extensive drawing office (left) worked on the latest designs. The result was the 'one-piece body', illustrated in this draft advertisement from 1930 (right).

The immense size of the equipment is well illustrated by the tiny figures of the two operators. Working at Pressed Steel was a dangerous job. Only a few of the sixty presses had guards and the working environment was hazardous and dirty.

The transition from traditional coach–building was gradual. Initially many of the panels pressed out by the new machines continued to skin the traditional ash frames, particularly for non-standard cars such as this Morris Ten, fitted out as a two–door coupé with rather exotic coachwork.

But assembly processes were steadily improving. These three workmen faced considerably less difficulty than their colleagues on page 54. A mechanical hoist made the procedure of guiding the body onto the chassis below both simpler and kinder to the back muscles.

Another production technique that came with the all-steel body was electronic welding. Not only was this quicker, it was also more consistent, providing the ability to repeat spot welds every few inches.

Sometimes it was still necessary, as part of the finishing process, to use a hand wheeling machine to ensure the correct curvature of the panel. Goggles were provided for eye protection.

Small adjustments had to be made to the bodies as they travelled along the line. A jack was used to tweak the body so the doors would close properly. The elaborate structure of the open door illustrates the difference between a hand-beaten and a stamped-out panel.

Pressed Steel also had its own paint shop and when a body left the works it was a complete unit ready to mount on the awaiting mechanical assembly.

At Pressed Steel as well as Morris Motors production methods continued to improve and by 1939 components were being joined together using hand-held welding guns which were suspended from overhead rails.

The development of the 'monocoque', which had a combined chassis and bodyshell, was the culmination of the all-steel body process. This Morris Ten Series M from 1938 was an early example. By the 1950s the majority of motor cars had this unitary structure.

Five
A Gift for Publicity

While equipping its assembly lines with the most up-to-date technology, Morris Motors sought to use the latest publicity techniques to attract customers to its products.

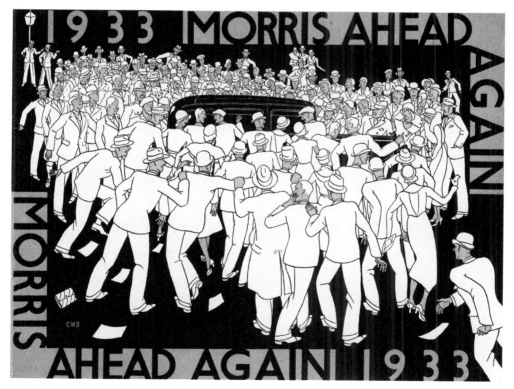

Morris Motors dealer brochure from 1933.

William Morris claimed to shun the advertising media, boasting that he never spent even a halfpenny on advertising between 1912 and 1918, as the cars sold themselves. In reality, he showed a gift for publicity from the very beginning. He was wise enough to advertise his cycle business in Kelly's Directory of Oxford and as a young man used his prowess at cycling to promote his business by always racing bicycles he had manufactured himself and winning numerous medals. When he moved into motor manufacture he rarely missed a promotional opportunity. In 1912 when he was just starting out in motor manufacture he provided dealers with free catalogues to encourage them to stock Morris cars. There were many other ways of advertising the product. Feats of endurance, for example, were very popular and the company encouraged all manner of adventurers to drive its products long distances through often hostile terrain to prove their worth.

It was in the early 1920s, however, that sales promotion began in earnest. Morris took on a young journalist called Miles Thomas, who had greatly impressed him with his articles about motoring. Their philosophy was that happy owners were the best advertisement for any product. By making customers feel good about the company, they could count on them spreading a favourable message about the cars. To this end in 1924 they launched a commercial journal, the *Morris Owner*, which celebrated the product and dispensed motoring advice. In a remarkably forward-thinking way it also invited participation from its readers by asking for their stories and holiday tales and this met with an enthusiastic response. Then, as now, the 'common man' liked to have his say! The magazine continued until 1951 and was much copied by rival firms.

To publish this new journal and to meet the growing requirement for other company litera-ture, the Morris Oxford Press (renamed the Nuffield Press in 1942) was established in 1925 to produce and print Morris publications. It was set up in the original part of the Cowley factory, the old Military College buildings, which were no longer suitable for manufacturing activities. Though the assembly halls had moved, Lord Nuffield did not and he kept his original office on the top floor of the Nuffield Press building until his death in 1963. It was preserved here as he left it until 1993, when the listed building was converted into luxury apartments as part of the redevelopment of the factory site. The office was reconstructed at the Heritage Motor Centre in Gaydon where it is now on display.

Cowley also established its own film unit with the most up-to-date film equipment and a fleet of Morris vans to carry crews on location. The 'Cine Department' spent a great deal of its time recording all aspects of factory life. Every opportunity was taken to show off the latest production techniques in use, because modern technology was perceived to mean the best product. These films were turned into short documentaries to keep distributors, dealers and customers informed about the latest developments at Cowley. There were also promotional films featuring the product range and William Morris himself was a frequent player in this earliest form of celluloid advertising.

From the start of his career William Morris understood the power of publicity. He used his skill as a cyclist to prove the value of his products, winning many racing medals in Oxfordshire, Berkshire and Buckinghamshire. In 1900 he secured seven championships while riding cycles he built himself and then declared his retirement. In 1904 he was challenged to defend the titles he had won from the now defunct East Oxford and Oxonian Cycling Clubs. With barely two weeks' notice, and reluctantly riding a machine he had not made himself, Morris claimed the trophies again, this time permanently.

William Morris (left) drafted in ambitious young journalist Miles Thomas (right) to spearhead the promotion of his products. In 1924 they posed with a Morris Oxford which had been driven by Mr Bowser (centre) from Land's End to John O'Groats without stopping the engine.

Morris Motors was not the only firm to realise the value of sponsorship. These two smartly dressed adventurers brought their car back to the factory in 1929. It was inscribed with a slogan which had informed passers-by that 'this Morris Cowley car going from Singapore to London overland is running entirely on Castrol motor oil and Dunlop tyres'.

MG was now a big name in the sporting world. In 1933 Morris was happy to pose with an MG Magnette which had been driven to victory in the Ulster TT race by famous racing driver Tazio Nuvolari.

Between the wars the economic climate was precarious. In 1931 Morris Motors produced a Morris Minor with a price tag of £100, the first British car to reach that magical price. This not only buoyed sales but also attracted a good deal of favourable publicity.

Keeping the customer happy. By now Morris Garages had many outposts and in 1923 the branch at Cornmarket Street in the city centre was offering a full range of customer services including tyre inflation at a cost 2d for a single tyre or 6d for all four. While waiting, the owner could muse on the sentiment 'Buy British and be proud of it'.

Inside the Morris Garages showroom at Queen Street, the customer could browse through Morris brochures in well-appointed surroundings. It was from this showroom that the first 'MG' car – a Morris with a highly tuned engine – was sold in 1924.

The repair shop of 1928 did not enjoy the advantages of hydraulic hoists and a system of winches and trestles was in use.

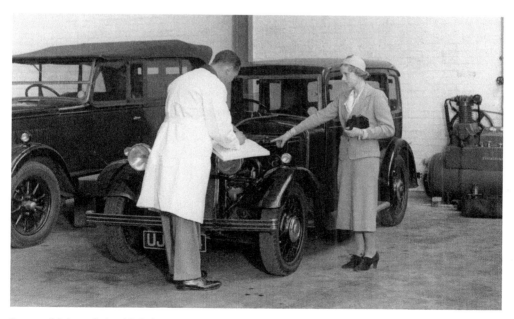

In 1937 this knowledgeable lady owner was presumably drawing the attention of the service engineer to the bald tyre on the passenger side of her car.

The showrooms of Morris Garages were known for their elegant window displays. This illuminating Exide batteries layout from 1929 includes a £1,000 limerick competition. Example rhymes are provided such as 'Joys of a night ride depend upon Exide'.

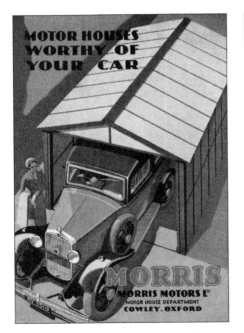

One of the more unusual accessories for a Morris car was the prefabricated Motor House (left), introduced in 1926. Distributors were also offered a range of signs (right), from the illuminated Bullnose radiator to the showroom barometer.

Miles Thomas masterminded the setting up of the company's own publishing arm, the Morris Oxford Press (renamed Nuffield Press in 1942). This took over the original Military College building for activities such as the collation of publicity material on the endless band conveyor.

Though manufacturing was relocated, Morris kept his office on the top floor of the Nuffield Press. This homely room, from its worn leather couch to its flooring made from bits of patched-together car carpet, provides a fascinating insight into the character of an eccentric millionaire.

The Morris Oxford Press became the centre of the entire publishing arm of the Nuffield empire, from typesetting …

… to the printing of the finished pages of thousands of magazines, handbooks, brochures, posters and many other types of company literature.

The *Morris Owner* (left), launched in 1924, was one of the earliest commercial journals produced by a British motor company and became very popular. Meanwhile, a 1930s sales brochure (above) promoted the idea of a progressive company prepared to 'look ahead', like its customers.

This futuristic poster captured the tone of advertising in this period, heralding the Morris as 'the perfect product of modern science'.

MORRIS "TALKIES"

TELL THE STORY TO YOUR CUSTOMERS

" Saying it with celluloid " is now recognised as the brightest and briskest way of selling cars, and Morris Motors Ltd. were the first to adopt " sound films," and their displays to-day are well to the fore for interest and sales value. In fact, so successful has this ultra-modern method of salesmanship proved itself that additional projection equipment is available for Morris Distributors and Dealers for the 1933 season.

The actual films and apparatus, the printed invitations and advertising material, and a special leaflet, " How to organise a Morris Sound Film Display," showing how simple a matter it is to give a really successful and profitable show, are all *entirely free*, and every possible assistance is given to make your particular show a complete success in every way.

They see the actual cars in comfort whilst you preside as host . . .

Cowley also led the way with its pioneering Cine Department. Distributors and dealers were encouraged to arrange special evening shows where their customers could enjoy 'talkies' about the company and its products – 'They see the actual cars in comfort while you preside as host'. Invitations, leaflets, the films and even sophisticated equipment such as the 'Kalee' projector being used by projectionist Mr Smith (bottom right) were all provided free of charge.

How best to demonstrate the excellence of the Morris car? What better than to subject a second-hand Isis saloon to a 'trial by ordeal'. First soak it in petrol, set fire to it and put out the flames. Then start it up and drive it through a brick wall. It will, of course, run perfectly, although as the commentator remarks, 'looking a trifle battered,' while the driver will still be able to dispense a cheery wave of the hand.

Photographed & Produced by
THE CINE DEPARTMENT AT COWLEY

William Morris often appeared in the films personally. Here the studio was set up for the latest car promotion and he pointed knowledgeably to some detail of the chassis for the benefit of the camera.

A Special Excursion to OXFORD has been arranged on

A VISIT TO THE COLLEGES & THE MORRIS WORKS

FULL PARTICULARS WITHIN

A trip to Cowley was as much a part of a tour of Oxford as the university. This 1938 poster emphasised the company at the expense of any other attraction, and doubtless hoped to find some new customers by impressing them with the magnificence of the Morris Works.

Six
Behind the Scenes

There was more to the life at a Nuffield factory than putting cars together. Many men and women were employed in the offices and the welfare of the workforce was a prime consideration, with a full range of health and leisure facilities on offer.

From the enquiry office a commissionaire observes an office worker hurrying by.

Over the years William Morris supported, founded and purchased numerous other companies throughout Oxford, Coventry and Birmingham. Names such as MG, Riley, and Wolseley would all come under the umbrella of the ever-growing Nuffield Organisation. Of course not everyone was employed directly on the assembly line, and the staff of the canteens and those who paid out the wages were just as vital in keeping production running smoothly. The huge number of people engaged 'behind the scenes' in areas such as administration, the surgeries and fire stations, the design studio, the chemical laboratories or the switchboard should not be forgotten.

Yet, while business success made Lord Nuffield a very wealthy man, his private life was notable for its lack of ostentation. He became legendary for his philanthropy and the value of his donations over his lifetime has been calculated at £30 million – a figure worth over ten times this amount in current values. He thought very carefully about each donation, determined that his money would make a real difference to people's lives, and also anxious to make a contribution to his home town of Oxford. He once said that it was more difficult to give money wisely than it was to make it. Most of his benefactions were to do with medicine. This was linked to the ill-health of his parents as well as his own unfulfilled ambition to be a doctor. He pioneered the manufacture of iron lungs and gave them away free to hospitals. There are still numerous research foundations and nursing homes graced with the name of Nuffield thanks to his generosity. This is apart from his gifts to Oxford University where he founded Nuffield College for the study of social science and also responded to an appeal for support from the small and recently founded St Peter's Hall nearby.

At the same time he made sure his factories catered for the welfare and safety of the workforce. Early in the 1920s a volunteer fire brigade was formed. Surgeries were set up for nurses and doctors and various kinds of medical check-ups were on offer. Pressed Steel too was at the forefront of health care for its employees, and the new works of 1926 incorporated a hospital where all types of ailment could be treated, mild or severe. Adjacent was a dentist's surgery, open to all workers in the hope that attention to oral hygiene would keep them away from their jobs for the minimum length of time.

Life away from work did not necessarily mean life away from Cowley. At a time when the attractions of the television and home computer did not exist, much of an employee's leisure time was provided for by the factory. Recreational activities were seen as an essential part of encouraging a productive workforce, creating a sense of community and pride. Lord Nuffield even provided an athletics ground complete with a fine clubhouse for the enjoyment of his workforce. The range of pursuits was broad, from the League of Health and Beauty to snooker, a brass band and a drama group. There was also a wide selection of competitive sports such as boxing, football, rugby, cricket, hockey or fishing. The factories of the Nuffield Organisation provided plenty of worthy opponents, and there were also opportunities to compete with other companies.

The Service Department handled many vehicles and a small office of staff maintained the index card system used to track jobs from start to completion.

An atmospheric photograph from 1923 – Cowley had a test laboratory to analyse materials of all sorts used in motor car production for quality.

The employee's favourite day of the week? On pay-day a temporary station was set up by the side of the track where administrative staff distributed the wage packets containing cash to factory and office workers.

Preparing these packets for thousands of workers was a laborious process, alleviated only slightly by automatic coin dispensing machines. It would be the 1970s before employers began to encourage the direct payment of salaries into bank accounts and many workers resisted the move.

The Morris Motors Cashier's Office was a hub of activity. The high chairs on which the cashiers were perched enabled them to look clients standing on the other side of the window in the eye.

It was not just the production lines which had their equipment constantly upgraded. By 1936 this administrator had a state-of-the-art calculator and a fully adjustable chair.

At the hub of the Cowley communications system, three telephonists operated the factory switchboard in 1944.

A Cowley commissionaire used an alternative method, the elaborate message chutes which were activated by compressed air. Morris Motors had a policy of employing some of the many people disabled in the First World War.

SOUVENIR PROGRAMME OF THE
MORRIS MOTORS
SPORTS MEETING

PRESIDENT AND PATRON · · · W. R. MORRIS, ESQ.

CRESCENT ROAD, COWLEY

Price Threepence

SATURDAY, JUNE 27TH, 1925

The sports meeting was an annual event, held at the playing fields on Crescent Road, adjacent to the original factory and site of the athletics pavilion provided by Nuffield himself. This colourful souvenir programme of 1925 is illustrated with a runner bearing a strong resemblance to its patron.

Above:
Inter-departmental rivalry was always a feature of factory social life. The winners of the 1925 tug of war competition from the Carpentry Department posed proudly with the rope and the victor's trophy.

Left: Aerobic exercise is no new thing: here the Women's League of Health and Beauty was going through its routine, following the lead of their instructor, Miss Mary Bell.

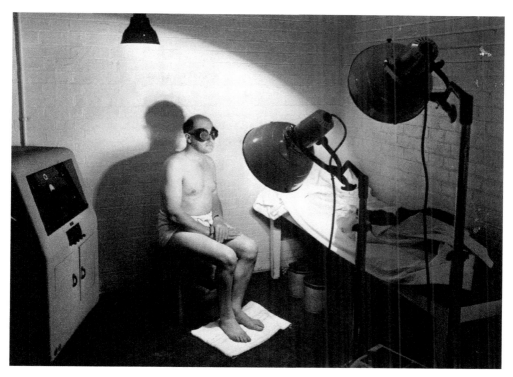

The war period was thought to have had a serious effect on the vitality of the population. In an attempt to revive the pallid workforce, employees were invited to make full use of the 'sunbath' treatment room. It looks rather intimidating for this factory worker in 1946.

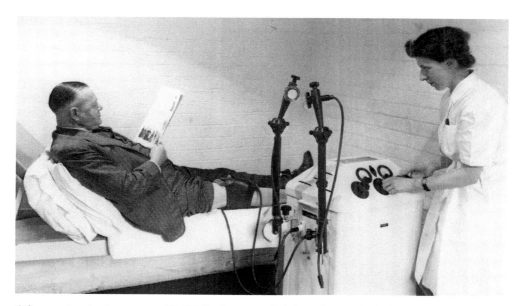

Other routine checks were on offer. While the nurse administered some physiotherapy to his knee, this patient was engrossed in his reading material. Hopefully it was a Morris magazine.

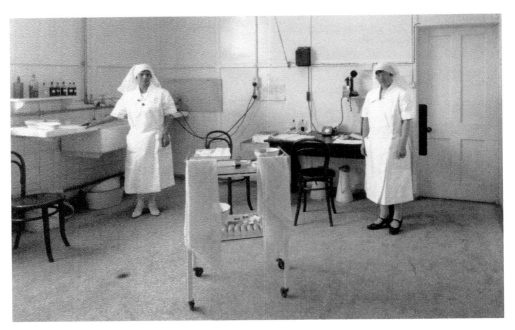

Pressed Steel contained comprehensive medical facilities including a surgery where two nurses awaited their next patient surrounded by an impressive array of equipment.

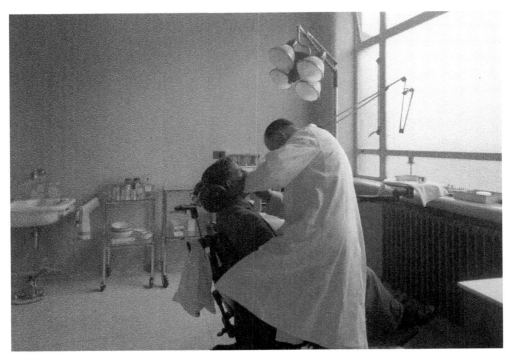

Dental services were also provided. Having a dentist's surgery minimised the time an employee needed to be away from work.

The inspiration behind Nuffield's interest in medicine was his family. His mother, Emily Ann Morris, suffered from heart and breathing problems. He continued to provide for her in old age and a portrait of her illustrious son hung on the wall behind her chair.

In 1938, on a visit to the Nuffield medical departments at Oxford University, Lord Nuffield saw a film about artificial respiration featuring the Both respirator. Inspired by its potential to save the lives of those suffering from diseases such as polio if used in time, he began a programme to build the 'iron lung' at Cowley.

By mass producing them, he was able to lower the cost to one-quarter of its previous figure and he distributed them free of charge to hospitals who applied for them. Here, the film unit captured the moment as Lord Nuffield himself made a presentation in 1938. When war stopped production just one year later more than 1,700 iron lungs had been made and given away.

Cartoonists continued to draw Nuffield, depicting Oxford dons eagerly receiving his bounty from 'the horn of plenty' (left). Though he left school at fourteen to go into trade, Morris received many academic honours beginning with an Hon DCL (Doctor of Civil Law) in 1931 from Oxford University (right).

He, in his turn, contributed much to the university which so dominated his home city. One of his benefactions was Nuffield College, depicted in this architect's model of 1954. He wanted to dedicate it to engineering but the Oxford hierarchy felt this would put them in competition with Cambridge so it became a centre for postgraduate study in the social sciences.

A well-trained fire brigade protected the workforce and also minimised risk to the large stocks of parts tied up in the factory.

A broad range of activities was available on the social side of factory life, such as this snooker table in the club room at the Morris Radiators Branch.

Lord Nuffield was a keen supporter of the Morris Motors Band which was very successful over the years, winning many competitions.

There were also opportunities for those with a theatrical inclination. The Morris Radiators staff displayed their acting talents in a 1959 production of *Sailor Beware*.

The works canteen provided sustenance for the workforce. The poster on the right-hand side of this 1925 photograph advertises the Morris Motors Band's next concert at Oxford Town Hall.

Catering was similarly an important part of social events. Here the Morris Radiators Branch cricket team members enjoyed their annual dinner in 1953.

Choose a chicken, any chicken! A fabulous display of poultry awaiting the 1929 Christmas draw.
Chicken was a luxury rather than an everyday food.

Not only did the canteen provide food, it advertised it too, in this case a comprehensive display of
Australian produce. Australia was one of Lord Nuffield's favourite holiday destinations though he is not
known to have favoured 'Emu wine' which was apparently 'good for you, good for the Empire'.

Pressed Steel set up a subsidiary, 'Prestcold', which was able to help out in the domestic kitchen too. This freezer from the 1960s was packed with 'Quick Frozen Food' products which look familiar, including fried potato chips, chicken pies and sausages.

The beginnings of the fitted kitchen can be seen in this combined steel sink, cupboard and cooker unit, also from Pressed Steel.

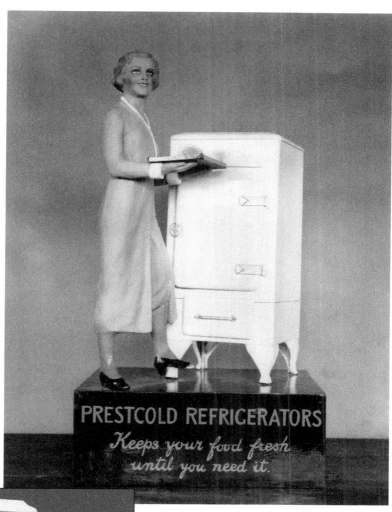

Above and left: The refrigerator had become an essential piece of equipment for every kitchen by the 1960s, but in the 1930s this rather scary plaster lady would have been very privileged to own such an item. The unit was something like a reverse Tardis, being much smaller on the inside than the outside.

Some decided to stock their freezers personally with a spot of fishing. The Morris Radiators Branch fishing club competed for the T.E. Rees Cup in 1964.

Seven
Second World War

The advent of the Second World War meant diversification into military hardware once again, though this time the motor industry was better prepared for what lay ahead.

Making an aeroplane fuselage at the Pressed Steel Works.

The Second World War represented another challenge to the industry, but now the factories of the Nuffield empire were well established they were capable of producing a much greater range of munitions and fighting machines than during the last war. Former Publicity Manager Miles Thomas had risen to become Vice-Chairman and he led the company through this difficult time, being rewarded with a peerage once the conflict was over. Cowley's main assembly building, 'C' block, was used as a military inspection area. 'G'-'K'-'N' block produced mines, trucks and light reconnaissance vehicles. Wings for the Horsa glider were made in the sawmill area, De Havilland wing units were constructed in 'B' block and power units for Lancaster and Beaufighter fighter aeroplanes came out of the office buildings in 'L' block.

Morris Industries Exports (MIE), a building of 50,000 square feet, had been constructed next to the railway station in 1933 to act as a distribution centre for the growing network of Morris companies and from 1942 this became an ideal facility for tank production. On the other side of Garsington Road, new buildings which would be known as 'South Works' were put up for aeroplane construction and repair. One of the earliest contracts was for the manufacture of complete Tiger Moths, an early example of mass production techniques being applied to aircraft. These rather old-fashioned biplanes were used by the RAF for training purposes. William Morris became very involved with the Civilian Repair Organisation (CRO) which consisted of 1,500 repair centres for damaged aircraft. As a result, the major part of South Works became the No 1 Civilian Repair Unit (CRU) and devoted its wartime effort to putting damaged fighter planes back into service.

More than three-quarters of the regular Cowley workforce was called away for active service. Nevertheless employment during the war years swelled to over 10,000, more than double the peacetime number. The figure for the Nuffield Organisation as a whole was 45,000. A great proportion of that number was women, one of the more notable being the Duke of Marlborough's daughter, Sarah Churchill, who was engaged in the production of brass shell casings. Nuffield also turned his philanthropy to the care of the forces and set up a number of rest centres for the benefit of servicemen and women on leave.

When the war was finally over much of the newly installed equipment became available for peacetime production. The aeroplane repair areas in South Works contained valuable presses which were immediately turned to good use when car production resumed in 1946. As well as organising military production, Miles Thomas had been nurturing a young designer called Alec Issigonis, who had been encouraged to turn his imagination to the company's return to peacetime production alongside his military design duties. He wasted no time in coming up with an innovative small car which would lead the company's post-war product range, the Morris Minor.

A woman hard at work at the Pressed Steel factory, welding a jerrycan.

Regular displays of war products showed how the Cowley factories supported the war effort. This display of Pressed Steel production gave a small example of more than £3 million-worth of war equipment produced by the tool department.

As in the First World War, standard munitions manufacture was carried out at Cowley including torpedoes for supply to the Admiralty.

From 1942 Morris Industries Exports (later called Nuffield Exports) was turned over to the production of tanks.

These Crusader tanks weighed twenty-four tons and carried six-pounder guns. Almost 650 tanks had been assembled by the end of hostilities.

Once again women were brought back to mainstream factory jobs. Here the turret section of a Crusader is being assembled.

Miles Thomas had now risen to the post of Vice-Chairman and played a key role in organising wartime production. On 8 May 1942 he triumphantly drove the first Crusader out of the factory. It was assembled from some 10,000 parts and took twelve days to put together.

Thomas was encouraging the budding talent of young designer Alec Issigonis. During wartime he turned his mind to a variety of unusual military vehicles such as this 'amphibious wheelbarrow' which was designed to operate on both land and water.

This was another amphibious vehicle, an armoured car known as the Salamander, being tested in a water tank in 1942.

During the Second World War several schemes were tried to combat petrol rationing. One idea was to fit cars with coal gas systems. The gas was stored in a rather cumbersome bag fitted to the roof of the vehicle, in this case a Morris Ten.

The aeroplane was to be a key player in this war and the Cowley factory played a full part in their repair and manufacture, including the final stages of applying camouflage paint.

Morris Motors' first large-scale contract was for the complete construction of Tiger Moth aircraft. They made forty each week for use by the RAF as part of their training programme.

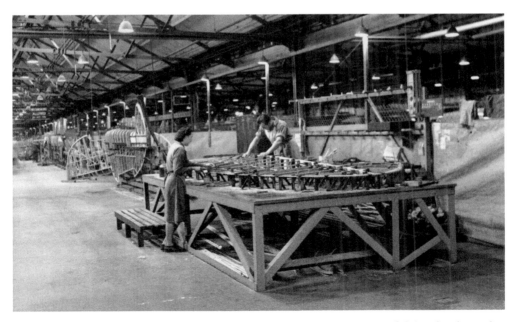

Cowley also built tail units for Horsa gliders. Even the time-consuming process of gluing the plywood skin onto the framework of the tail got the Morris treatment. By judicious use of clamps and inflated bicycle inner tubes, the lengthy task of pin-tacking the tail section to hold it in place until the glue had dried was avoided.

Lord Nuffield became closely involved with the Civilian Repair Organisation (CRO) which comprised 1,500 Civilian Repair Units (CRUs) of which Cowley was known as No 1 CRU. He often visited the aero-engine shed to discuss the work required with his labour force.

The role of the CRU was to strip and repair salvaged aeroplanes like this badly damaged Hurricane fighter.

By the end of 1945 the unit had handled over 75,000 aircraft repairs. Any components past repair were stripped down and used to produce new parts.

Nuffield set up canteens and leisure facilities to support members of the armed forces. This picture bore the caption, 'An ATS girl taking the 2,750,000th meal', an impressive number supplied at Lord Nuffield's expense.

With the war finally over, the RAF transported the remaining parts of wrecked aeroplanes away from Cowley to be scrapped.

It was time to think about car production again. Two storemen were sent to a Garsington Road lock-up to examine a consignment of packaged bumpers.

Towards the end of the war Alec Issigonis was released from the burden of designing and testing amphibious wheelbarrows to concentrate on a new model for the post-war period. The Mosquito was the prototype for the Morris Minor and was pictured in 1944 outside the camouflaged factory.

Eight
Post-War Boom, Takeover and Merger

In the last decade of his life Lord Nuffield found himself reunited with his former colleague and latter-day rival, Leonard Lord. This was because, in 1952, the Nuffield Organisation merged with the Austin Motor Company to create the British Motor Corporation (BMC) which would be a dominant force for the next sixteen years.

Lord Nuffield and Sir Leonard Lord greet each other at a celebratory dinner.

The car market in Britain immediately after the war was dominated by post-war austerity and a government-led initiative to promote exports which could earn badly needed foreign currency. Nuffield sought to exploit the situation by setting up foreign assembly plants in countries such as Australia, India and South Africa. By 1950, the level of Morris exports had quadrupled from its immediate pre-war figure and Cowley expanded in response. In 1949, further rebuilding and modernisation was undertaken which made a 30 per cent increase in output possible. South Works experienced the biggest expansion with a series of new buildings which were initially used for storage and the production of CKD (complete knock down) kits for export.

In 1946 it was pre-war products like the Morris Eight which went straight back into production as this was the quickest way to get civilian cars back onto the road. Spearheading the company's post-war effort was the innovative Morris Minor, a small car designed by Alec Issigonis, part of a product range which included the Morris Oxford, Morris Six, Wolseley 6/80 and Wolseley 4/50. Lord Nuffield disliked the Minor and wanted to carry on with a revised Morris Eight. His Vice-Chairman Miles Thomas engaged in a long battle with him over the issue, which he won before resigning and leaving the company for good. Launched to great acclaim in 1948, the success of this modern small car led to the conversion of part of South Works to accommodate a new manufacturing facility for its construction.

The future of Cowley, however, was about to be redefined by merger between the big rivals, the Nuffield Organisation and the Austin Motor Company, based at Longbridge, near Birmingham. Leonard Lord had already suggested this move to his former boss in the late 1940s, but Lord Nuffield had not been keen. A strong challenge to British manufacturers, however, was coming from both America and Europe, who were similarly trying to build up their export bases in an effort to recover from the economic damage suffered during wartime. By 1952 merger seemed the only sensible course of action and the grand marriage to form the British Motor Corporation (BMC) was finally effected. After a year Lord Nuffield took the honorary title of President and effectively went into retirement, though he still carried out publicity duties for the new corporation, being photographed with new models which were even less to his taste than the Morris Minor had been. Leonard Lord became Chairman with George Harriman as his deputy, and Harriman succeeded him when he finally retired in 1961.

At first Cowley seemed destined to be the inferior partner and there was a halt to expansion while a flurry of building activity took place on the Longbridge site. The largest investment of the BMC period was 'E' block which provided a new paint facility, rotodip body preparation plant and body store. In 1954, an overhead conveyor was stretched across the Oxford Eastern bypass, eliminating the need to take bodies by truck across the road. In 1955 Issigonis, who had briefly left the company in 1952, returned to become BMC's chief designer. His Mini, which was produced in Austin and Morris versions, came out in 1959. For ten years production was split between Longbridge and Cowley, though the latter produced much smaller volumes. But the product which would dominate Cowley during the late 1960s and early 1970s was another Issigonis design, the larger 1100, which became a best-selling family car.

Immediate post-war production was hampered by difficulties with component supply. These stockpiled bodies awaited the delivery of sufficient engines and other parts before they could be completed.

When car manufacture resumed it was based on pre-war models such these Morris Eights until new models were available.

The national slogan was 'export or die' and the home market was deliberately restricted to bring in foreign currency. The Nuffield Organisation turned its eyes to markets such as India by producing vehicles like the 'Hindustan' (based on the Morris Ten) and encouraging their local assembly.

But new models were finally on the way. The Morris Minor was designed by Alec Issigonis as part of the brand new model range, launched in 1948.

Lord Nuffield wanted to continue with an updated Morris Eight but he was finally persuaded that the company's future depended on introducing the Issigonis Morris Minor. To mark the change-over, bodyshells representing old and new were decorated with a wreath in the shape of an '8'.

Nevertheless Nuffield never concealed his dislike of the car he christened 'the poached egg' and he hated being photographed with it. He stared gloomily at the engine, the only thing to recommend it in his eyes since the Minor was initially fitted with the power unit from his preferred Morris Eight.

This Morris Minor bodyshell from Pressed Steel was a fine example of the unitary structure which was now becoming standard. Much to its designer's annoyance the headlamp position, originally integral with the grille, was raised to comply with US regulations.

This change enabled the Morris Minor to maintain its place in the export programme and 'Nuffield Exports' transporters were loaded with completed cars for their journey to the port.

A familiar view at Cowley. Workers left the factory gates for home in 1950, the majority still on bicycles, just as they had been in the 1930s.

1952 was a significant year for Morris Motors when it merged with its great rival, the Austin Motor Company, to form the British Motor Corporation (BMC). These certificates were issued to formalise the share transfer between old and new companies.

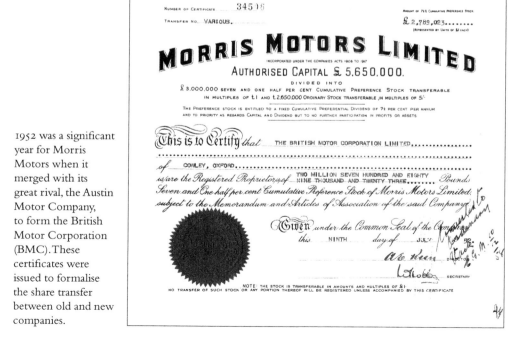

BMC took great pride in its testing procedures. At the end of the production line Morris Minor Travellers underwent rigorous checks for headlamp beam and wheel alignment not to mention the 'bump test'. Though the march of the pressed steel process had largely eliminated wooden frames, the Traveller was one of the last vehicles to be based extensively on a such a structure.

The noise levels generated by the engine of the Morris Oxford were also measured.

In the 'Zero F' chamber a Morris Oxford Series II and its intrepid driver were subjected to intense cold.

At the other end of the scale, the 'Tropical Room' explored the Morris Minor's resilience to extreme heat.

Before despatch, all cars were subjected to a final inspection. Here, Farina-styled MG Magnettes plus Morris pickups and vans sat on adjoining lines in 1959.

Pressed Steel still played an important role, supplying all the major British motor car manufacturers with bodies. They could either supply bodyshells bare like the Morris Minor on page 118, or trimmed and painted like these Hillman Minxes bound for the Rootes factory at Ryton in Coventry.

The 1950s was a period of great productivity and the Drawing Office was in full swing sketching out the many designs of the new corporation.

In 1959 Lord Nuffield (third from left) attended the London Motor Show along with Leonard Lord's deputy, George Harriman (fourth from left). They were looking at another revolutionary Issigonis design which, from his expression, seems to have impressed him as much as the 1948 Morris Minor.

The car was being marketed as the Morris Mini-Minor and the Austin Seven, though it would later become known as the Mini. Perhaps the reason for Lord Nuffield's frown was the fact that he was being shown a cutaway of the Austin, rather than the Morris version.

Fifties style! This young man was fitting the rear window trim to a Mini which was now taking over the mantle of pioneering technology from the Morris Minor.

Nevertheless the Morris Minor became the first British vehicle to reach a production figure of one million in 1960. To celebrate, a limited edition of 350 was produced in a fetching shade of lilac. According to Issigonis, Lord Nuffield actually thanked him when this landmark was reached!

For ten years the Mini was assembled at both Cowley and Longbridge. In spite of carrying both Austin and Morris badges, the two versions were not split between factories. The first and third cars are Morris Mini-Minors whilst the second and fourth are Austin Sevens. How to tell them apart? By the different radiator grilles and bonnet badges.

Issigonis followed the Mini in 1962 with the slightly larger 1100 which was to become a best-selling family car. Largely designed there, it became the mainstay of Cowley production. At Pressed Steel a group of apprentices put the finishing touches to a fine model of the bodyshell.

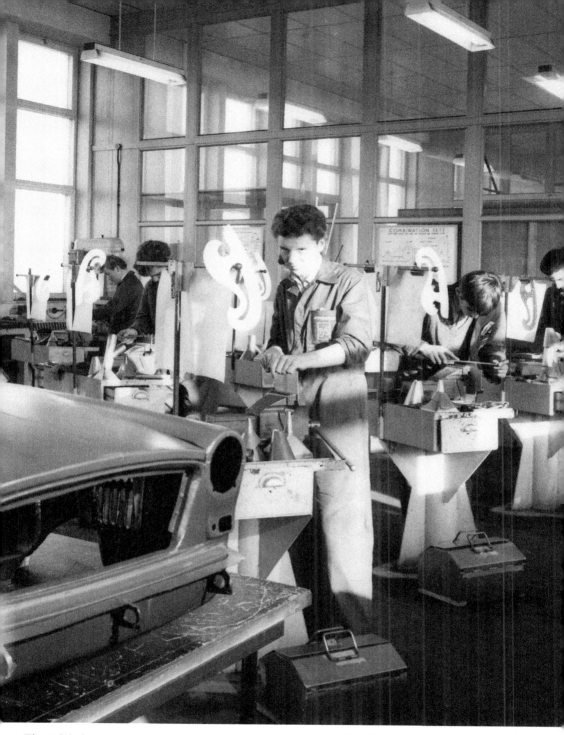

The stylish shape was created not by Issigonis, with his taste for simplicity, but by the Italian design house of Pininfarina. Though the result was less long-lived than the Mini, it was more in tune with contemporary tastes and contributed greatly to the car's popularity.

The acrobatics of the elegant 1100. First it pirouettes on the Rotodip. This process, introduced in the 1950s, consisted of a large bar inserted through the body which was then rotated as on a spit during the cleaning and painting processes ...

... then it dives up and down to shake itself dry before progressing further through the paint shop.

Once again, Lord Nuffield was persuaded to pose with an Issigonis design, in this case a Morris 1100 at its launch in 1962.

But this was the car he preferred, his special Wolseley Eight saloon, a prototype built in 1939, which he continued to use as his personal car until his death in 1963.

Modern technology was becoming ever more dominant. The assembly lines were now controlled remotely using punch cards.

A typical office scene in 1965. Regimented rows of desks were presided over by a stern office supervisor.

Over at Morris Radiators in 1960, production continued in a less high-tech environment as ashtrays were hot-dipped by hand to chromium plate them.

BMC Service at Cowley, set up in the mid-1960s, contained a vast store for the stockpiling of many components.

The operator was dwarfed by his vast console as he controlled the conveyor which moved parts around the store.

Controlling the store's operations was a series of impressive computer stations. Convincing customers that the company could supply parts efficiently was essential to BMC's strategy in the face of ever stronger competition from abroad.

Quality was the other key issue so inspectors were brought in to scrutinise the parts. The slickness of their work is matched by the shine of the Brylcreem liberally applied to their hair.

The final design from Issigonis in the BMC era was the 1800, the largest of his family of cars. It was only assembled at Cowley for a brief period before production was concentrated at Longbridge in 1967.

As the BMC era drew to a close, Cowley received a visit from the head of the Conservative Party and Leader of the Opposition, Edward Heath, though he arrived, rather disappointingly, in a Ford.

Nine
Mechanisation:
From BL to BMW

In 1968 British Leyland came into being and there was renewed activity to create a competitive model range, but crisis seemed to dog the company. Some success came from collaboration with Honda during the 1980s. Takeover by BMW in 1994 would lead to a new phase in Cowley's manufacturing history.

A demonstration of the art of clay modelling on the Montego to a group of enthralled youngsters in 1984.

There was more organisational upheaval during the 1960s. In 1966 BMC joined with Jaguar and Pressed Steel to form British Motor Holdings (BMH). In 1968, BMH in turn merged with the Leyland Motor Corporation, which included Standard-Triumph and Rover, to form the British Leyland Motor Corporation (BL). The organisation was headed by the former Leyland Chairman, Donald Stokes, and 'Morris' became one marque among the many owned by BL. The first post-merger volume model and the last Issigonis design was the Austin Maxi, launched in 1969. Despite its 'Austin' badge, it was to be built only at Cowley.

By 1971 BL was ready to launch the first of the models created by its own design team and the Morris Marina joined the Maxi. The Corporation, however, was beginning to struggle. In 1975 the government took a majority shareholding as a result of the Ryder Report, which had given a disturbing account of its economic condition. In 1977, Michael Edwardes was appointed Chairman and rationalised both production and the workforce at all BL's factories. After a long period of stagnation in the product range, work finally began in earnest on new designs and both Longbridge and Cowley were upgraded with robotic technology to manufacture them. While Longbridge received the first model, the much heralded Austin Metro, Cowley was to build the two larger cars, the Austin Maestro and Austin Montego. To make space for them the Morris Marina, now renamed Ital, was moved to Longbridge before being discontinued in 1984, the last car to bear the Morris name.

At the same time Edwardes commenced a joint venture with Honda of Japan. The first fruit of this was the Triumph Acclaim in 1981 and Cowley had the honour of building it. The Rover 800 followed in 1986. BL appeared to be on the road to recovery. By 1988 it had been renamed Rover Group and sold back into the private ownership of British Aerospace. This era would witness the most significant changes to the Cowley landscape since the original growth of the factory. In 1993 North and South Works, which were becoming difficult to upgrade with the most modern equipment, were demolished and replaced with the 'Oxford Business Park'. Because it was a listed building, the Military College exterior survived as part of a new complex of apartments. Production was concentrated on the former Pressed Steel site where some of the original buildings remained while others were redeveloped.

In 1994 the factory changed owners once again when Rover Group was bought by BMW of Bavaria. They invested over £700 million in the Cowley plant, installing the latest technology in preparation for the launch of the Rover 75 in 1998. A small car, to be sold under the name of MINI, was being designed for assembly at Longbridge. In 2000, however, BMW made a sudden decision to cut back its British operation. Longbridge was sold to a private consortium and the Rover 75, which had not lived up to their sales expectations, was included in the deal. Cowley was retained and turned over to the manufacture of the MINI, which became such a sales success for the German company that it would spawn a series of new models and variants in the following years. This secured many British jobs in the motor industry, whose traditional base had otherwise suffered so many setbacks during the first few years of the twenty-first century.

In 1968 BMC joined with Leyland Motor Corporation to form the British Leyland Motor Corporation (BL). Its chairman was Sir Donald Stokes, who joined Sir Alec Issigonis and Lord Snowdon at the opening of an exhibition of the BMC designer's sketches in 1971.

One of BL's first products was to be the last Issigonis design to reach production, the Austin Maxi, launched in 1969. The Maxi was not a sales success and Stokes promoted his right-hand man, Harry Webster, to begin work on BL's own designs.

In 1971 the conveyor bridge across the Oxford Eastern bypass was upgraded. Though this was intended to facilitate the transport of the first of the new models – the Morris Marina – it also transported the survivors from the previous model range, in this case the Maxi.

Despite the modernity of the conveyor, many assembly methods had still not moved on from manual processes, such as this windscreen fit on the Morris Marina.

At the end of the line an inspector performed some final checks on a completed Marina. The open bonnet illustrates the simplicity of the engine-bay layout which was designed to make the cars easier to maintain in contrast to the compact but complex arrangement of the later Issigonis designs.

In 1968 Pressed Steel had been merged with Fisher & Ludlow to become Pressed Steel Fisher. At their Cowley plant in 1971, Morris Marina bodies glided rather mysteriously towards a coat of paint.

The bodyshell had to be 'flatted' or sanded down in between the several coats of paint which it would receive. Once again, this was done by hand.

A workman filled his paint pot from a vat of red paint, one of the many bright colours which would grace the British Leyland product range through the 1970s.

Fitting a vinyl roof to the Wolseley 18/22 'wedge'. This was the height of fashion in 1975, the year of this picture sequence. Struck by an identity crisis, six months later the car became the 'Princess HLS' but kept its trendy roof.

That this was also 1975 is evident in the fashionable hairstyles whose proud owners were undoubtedly wearing flares as they welded together body panels for the 'wedge'.

The Princess attracted some lively advertising, though the heels of this model in 1978 were unlikely to have been good for the paintwork.

By the late 1970s Stokes had been replaced by trouble-shooter Sir Michael Edwardes. BL needed a partner to go forward and it was a significant moment when he and Mr Kawashima of Honda waved each other's national flag to celebrate the collaboration agreement signed in 1979.

The first result was the Triumph Acclaim, based on the Honda Ballade, built at Cowley from 1981.

As well as new products, the Japanese partners introduced new assembly methods. Engines and suspension were installed in the Acclaim from underneath the car, a process inelegantly known as the 'stuff up' method.

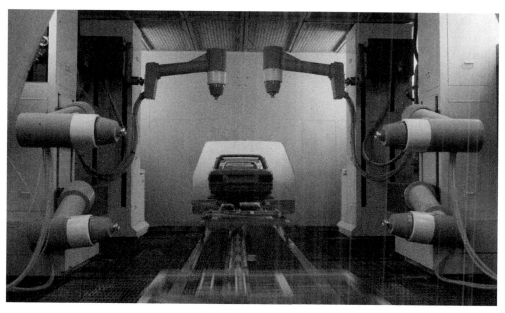

A brand new paint facility was installed for the Acclaim and for other models which were about to come on stream.

By 1983 Austin Rover's body engineering department had a bank of electronic machines operating the most recent 'Computer Aided Design' (CAD) programmes in place of rows of drawing boards.

As the first new British-designed model for eight years to come out of Cowley, the Maestro was an important vehicle and its assembly was heavily automated. As the cars neared completion they were subjected to a Vehicle Electrical Test System with the results displayed on overhead screens.

A big investment was made into Cowley for the Maestro and the brightly painted cars pouring off the end of the line at the final 'Quality Station' had progressed past fourteen robots capable of welding five different body styles. More than 60 per cent of the spot welds on the body were applied by a robot.

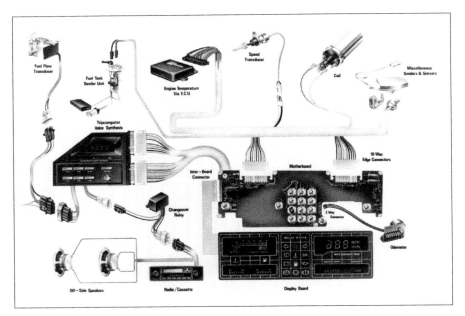

One gimmick on the top-of-the-range Maestro was the 'talking dashboard' which required extensive circuitry to do what could be achieved by a single silicon chip by the year 2000. In Britain the audio effects were provided by actress Nicolette McKenzie, after extensive market research to discover the most pleasing voice to customers.

Nicolette issued comforting advice about seat belts and fuel levels, complementing the modern look of the digital dashboard inside the car, which provided an additional range of helpful information. While certain voice commands could be overridden, on priority warnings she could not be silenced.

The Maestro was soon joined by the Austin Montego, which can be seen on the podium behind the designer working at this CAD station.

Early Montegos also had the talking dashboard option, but by 1988 this 2-litre GSi estate version was relying on cute cuddly toys to bring in the customers. The seven-seat estate version was a forerunner of the 'people carrier' of today.

In 1986 the Rover 800 came on stream, an executive car briefly sold in the USA as the 'Sterling'. The Honda Legend, on which it was based, was also built at Cowley for European markets. That year BL became Rover Group following the decision to concentrate on the Rover marque.

One of the processes designed to raise production quality was the injection of rust-proofing wax. Health and Safety regulations now provided the operatives with ear protectors (top picture), and a cap, gloves and face mask (above), in contrast to their predecessors.

An automatic framing station put together the body assembly of a Rover 800. Everything from positioning to welding was now done automatically.

Look no hands. By 1986 even the fitting of windscreen glass could be completed without manual assistance.

The relationship with Honda brought with it a new emphasis on quality control. A team of inspectors went over every last detail of this Rover 800 bodyshell in the quest for customer satisfaction.

Prime Minister Margaret Thatcher was equally keen to inspect Rover 800 quality. Not known to be a fan of British Leyland, she listens intently to Austin Rover's Chairman Harold Musgrove, but gives little clue about her thoughts to her husband Denis or the media pack behind.

It was becoming increasingly difficult to upgrade the old Morris Motors buildings with the latest technology. The owners at the time, British Aerospace, concluded that they had to go. The workers marked this key moment by posing with the last vehicles built before South Works was closed for demolition on 23 December 1992.

In 1993 South and North Works made way for a business park. Like monuments to the production line, the structures that carried the body conveyor remained standing for a brief time above the demolition. Car production continued on the former Pressed Steel site.

British Aerospace sold Rover Group to BMW in 1994. They invested a substantial sum in readiness to replace the Honda-derived designs with their own large car in 1998.

This model was the Rover 75, a luxurious saloon with retro styling which was to be built exclusively at Cowley. It encapsulated BMW's interpretation of the brand values of the Rover marque.

FIRST MINI OF THE
NEW MILLENIUM

BMW was also planning to use the MINI brand on a new small car. Though it was mostly designed at Longbridge, and was intended to be manufactured there, some of the body development took place at Cowley, where this picture was taken in 1999. This group contained members of the teams from both factories. When BMW changed its plans in 2000, scaling down its British operations, Longbridge was sold to a local consortium and allowed to take with it the Rover 75, whose sales had been disappointing. The deal meant that, unexpectedly, MINI came to Cowley.

In 1968, when it was still in its infancy, British Leyland emblazoned the walls below the sloping roofs of the factory with a bold message 'There's no Mini like the new Mini'. Underneath sat some other Issigonis designs, a Morris Minor and the Riley 'Kestrel' version of the 1100.

By 2006 a new MINI was firmly installed at Cowley and had become a big success for its owners, BMW. An example clung to the wall of the old Pressed Steel building, along with its slogan 'MINI Adventure Inside'.

Ten
A Car Named Morris
1913–84

When William Morris assembled his first vehicle at The Morris Garage in 1913, he was one of the youngest entrepreneurs to enter what was, by then, an established industry. His achievements would, nevertheless, outlast many who had entered the trade of motor manufacture before him. As well as the many factories he founded, the manufacturing methods he pioneered and the generous benefactions which his success as a businessman made possible, he would also enjoy the distinction of having his name attached to a succession of well-loved models until the Morris marque went out of use seventy-one years later, in 1984.

The Morris Oxford, with its distinctive 'bullnose' radiator, photographed in 1925.

The Morris Oxford, William Morris' first car design back in 1913, would be the first production car to bear a Morris badge. It was joined by a cheaper version called the Morris Cowley in 1915. Both featured a distinctive cowled radiator which became known as a 'bullnose' until 1927, when the 'flatnose' radiator was introduced. Early Morris cars generally followed the contemporary convention of model-naming by using a number related to the horsepower of the engine: Eight, Ten, Twenty and so on. Those which varied from this practice reflected Lord Nuffield's attachment to his native county: Oxford, Cowley or Isis, for example. A new small car joined the family in 1929, the Morris Minor. In a variation on the horsepower theme, 'Minor' reflected the size of the car, which was introduced to compete with the best-selling Austin Seven.

The period following the Second World War would see motor manufacturers seeking to modernise their designs, though many of them clung to the familiarity of pre-war names. The first new model to come from the Nuffield Organisation in 1948 was an entirely new Morris Minor. This would become one of Britain's best loved cars, surviving for an impressive twenty-four years in production. Designed by Nuffield's talented engineer Alec Issigonis, it was soon followed by the Morris Oxford and the Morris Six.

Lord Nuffield's habit of acquiring rival companies and creating new ones meant that 'Morris' quickly became one of a selection of marques available, alongside MG, Riley and Wolseley. When the Nuffield Organisation joined up with the Austin Motor Company as the British Motor Corporation in 1952, the two companies possessed an even longer list between them. Nevertheless, the Morris marque survived, though often on badge-engineered cars such as the 'Farinas' which began to launch in 1958. The point of badge-engineering was to appeal to the perceived brand loyalty of the British public and for the same reason some of the old model names, such as Oxford, Cowley and Isis, were also revived. Longest to survive was the Oxford, which stayed in use until the Series VI went out of production in 1971, well into the British Leyland era. The first truly original BMC model was the Morris Mini-Minor which would go on to become known simply as Mini. The medium-sized 1100 followed, launched as a Morris in 1962 one year ahead of the Austin version. It was this car rather than the Mini which would be the best-seller of the 1960s.

When British Leyland was formed in 1968 it was decided to focus on two entirely new models to replace the ageing product range. One would be a Morris, the other an Austin, breaking with the tradition of badge-engineering. The Morris Marina was launched first, to much fanfare, in 1971, followed by the Austin Allegro in 1973. With a very short development period of only three years and utilising some of the engineering from the Issigonis Morris Minor, this car was intended as a short-term fix until something better could be produced. Events, however, overtook British Leyland and the Marina design would stay in production much longer than intended, the backbone of the product range for the next thirteen years. Its successor, the re-styled Morris Ital, would mark the last appearance of the Morris badge on a production car and it fell out of use for good at the end of 1984.

This advertising hoarding is an example of numerous selling aids distributed to the extensive dealer network. It depicts the Morris Cowley, a cheaper version of the Oxford due to its more austere specification, but with the same distinctive 'bullnose' radiator.

In 1927 the 'flatnose' radiator was introduced. This is a four-seater Morris Cowley tourer, whose smartly dressed occupants are enjoying a picnic in the countryside.

In 1929 the Morris Minor was introduced. It was not able to overtake the popularity of the Austin Seven in the small-car market. Nevertheless, in the battle between manufacturers amidst a deep economic recession, it would become the first car with a price tag of only £100.

Fuel economy was a key selling point. After Peter Becke (extreme left) achieved 100 miles per gallon with his Morris Minor special in 1931, he brought the car to Cowley where Leonard Lord and Sir William Morris were among the interested onlookers.

At the top end of the model range were grander cars such as the Morris Isis (here in 1933). This was another Oxford reference: 'Isis' was the name given to the River Thames above Iffley Lock, where the university's rowers often practised.

Long-distance expeditions were another way of gaining publicity. This Morris Twenty-Five travelled across the Sahara desert in 1935, attracting curious crowds along the way.

THE NEW
MORRIS *EIGHT*
AS BIG AS AN ORDINARY TEN

The Morris Eight was introduced in 1934 and would rapidly succeed where the Minor had failed by overtaking the Austin Seven as Britain's best-selling small car. This Series I brochure illustration from 1935 emphasises the spaciousness of the four-door saloon.

Morris was also known for commercial vehicles like this 8/10cwt van. Painted in the livery of Sillers, makers of 'baby cars' (better known as prams) and 'invalid furniture', the vehicle is loaded up for a delivery outside its premises in Leeds on a wet winter's day.

The slightly larger Morris Ten was a staple of the model range. Two women have parked their saloon at a local beauty spot in the Gloucestershire village of Bibury in the Cotswolds in 1937.

By 1939, as the Second World War approached, the Morris Eight Series E had become a worldwide success. This export model belongs to a proud father who displays its practicality for his large family of seven, made up of the baby in his arms and the six children in their fez hats who surround him.

Britain declared war on Germany on 3 September 1939. This illustration, featured on the front cover of the *Morris Owner* for December 1939, depicts a poignant scene which would soon become all too familiar. An officer says a sad goodbye to his wife as he departs for the front line to do his duty. His chauffeur carries his luggage to the Morris car sitting outside their country cottage on a snowy winter's day. Production of civilian cars would be halted until the second major conflict of the twentieth century was over, but once again Morris vehicles would play an important part in the campaign. The car has a blackout shield on one of its headlamps; blackout regulations would lead to many deaths on Britain's roads.

The first new design after the war was the Morris Minor Series MM whose name harked back to the pre-war era. Aimed at the export market, this tourer had a 1949 US specification, including the raised headlight modification which so displeased its designer, Alec Issigonis.

A Morris Minor 1000 on the streets of Oxford in 1957. A police motorcyclist politely explains the significance of yellow lines to an elderly couple.

Issigonis also designed a new Morris Oxford. The first version was the Series MO, launched in 1948, but this illustration is from the brochure for the Series II version of 1953.

The post-war Oxford would become the most long-lived Morris car of all. In 1954 the design was licensed to Hindustan Motors and in 1957 the tooling was transferred to their factory at Uttarpara in West Bengal, India. This scene is from the 1974 brochure for the Hindustan Ambassador, as the Indian version was named. The Ambassador was still in production in 2013, Morris' centenary year.

The first all-new model to be launched by BMC in 1959 was the Morris Mini-Minor (also available as an Austin Seven) designed by Alec Issigonis. Its advertising slogan, 'Wizardry on Wheels', reflected its innovation. The badges harked back to the most famous pre-war Morris and Austin small cars, but the word 'Mini' had to be added to the Morris version to distinguish it from the Issigonis Morris Minor, which was still in production. Ironically this incidental word would eventually displace the unwieldy 'official' names and in 1969 the Morris and Austin badges were dropped altogether. This Morris Mini-Minor was photographed at the Cowley shopping centre in 1965.

The Farinas modernised the older cars in the model range without expensive re-engineering – 'inspiration from Farina, reliability from Morris'. In this 1961 workshop a Morris Oxford Series V receives attention from a mechanic, while Rileys and Austins can be seen in the background.

The Mini soon became a glamorous must-have for the fashionable set, none more so than the Mini Cooper S Mark 2, here in its Morris version in 1968.

Issigonis followed the Mini with the 1100, launched first as a Morris in 1962. It featured an advanced 'Hydrolastic' suspension system and styling by Pininfarina. A 1965 publicity shot in the Lake District portrays its less trendy, more homely image.

The police 'Panda' car, so called because of the pattern of its livery, was introduced as a local patrol vehicle in the mid-1960s. The 1100 – in this case a Mark 2 from 1969 – was one of a range of family cars used for making routine checks on venues such as this neighbourhood cinema.

The Morris Minor and commercial vehicles both continued to be important elements of the BMC model range. They combine here as a Post Office telephone van servicing a traditional red phone box in the suburbs during 1965.

The 1800, the largest car in the Issigonis model range, was launched in 1964 as an Austin. The Morris version was available from 1966, briefly built at Cowley during 1966–67. This early Morris 1800 is a visitor to the Oxford University Rugby Club whose home ground was on Iffley Road.

In 1968 the Morris marque became part of British Leyland, which was anxious to get some new designs on the market. The Morris Marina was launched in 1971 under the slogan 'beauty with brains behind it', which would appear to be the not-too-subtle message of this publicity shot.

A Marina 1.8 SDL Estate of 1973 with an average seventies family. Though the car never challenged the hugely popular Ford Cortina in the fleet market as hoped, it was nevertheless a remarkable success for a car which was only ever intended to be a temporary stopgap in the model range.

THE 18·22 SERIES. The car that's got it all together.

The Austin/Morris 18/22 series, here in its Morris version, was introduced in 1975. This was a last flourish for badge-engineering. After only six months 'the car that's got it all together' lost its marque designations and was rebadged as the 'Princess'.

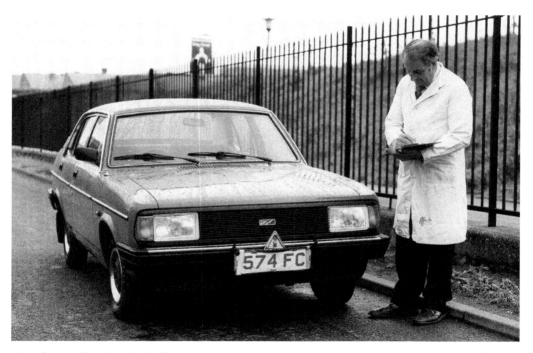

In July 1980 British Leyland relaunched the Marina as the Morris Ital, which it claimed was 'styled in Italy, built in Britain'. Though the body-tooling was undertaken by Giorgetto Giugiaro's Italdesign studio, located in Moncalieri near Turin, it was actually styled by Austin Rover's design team at Longbridge. This Ital has just returned on trade plates from a rainy test session.

Assembling the Morris Ital at Cowley in 1980. Manufacture was transferred to Longbridge in 1982 to make way for the Maestro. The Ital would be the last production car to carry a Morris badge. The saloon, van and estate car were all discontinued during 1984. Austin Rover believed that the name had become associated in the public mind with light commercials, so it was briefly retained on a Morris Metro van, but by the end of 1984 the marque had been dropped completely after seventy-one years of continuous use.

If you enjoyed this book, you may also be interested in…

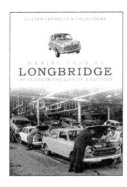

Making Cars at Longbridge
GILLIAN BARDSLEY & COLIN CORKE

Containing unique images from the official company archive, this book charts almost 100 years of car-making at Longbridge near Birmingham. The Austin Motor Company was founded here by Herbert Austin in 1905 and it has since been home to the British Motor Corporation, British Leyland, Rover Group and latterly MG Rover. Its products include some of the most famous British models ever produced: the pioneering Austin Seven, the classic Mini, the Austin Metro, and in later years the best-selling MG TF and elegant Rover 75.

978-0-7524-3741-0

The Mini Story
GILES CHAPMAN

The 1959 Mini set the template from which all successful compact cars have been created. The original Mini was on sale for 41 years, during which its 5.3 million sales made it the best-selling British car of all time – an achievement unlikely ever to be beaten. And just when it looked like the little car would shrivel and die, BMW reinvented it as the planet's most desirable small car range, and put it back on the serious motoring map as the MINI.

978-0-7524-6282-0

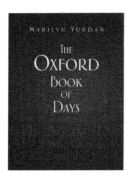

The Oxford Book of Days
MARILYN YURDAN

Taking you through the year day by day, *The Oxford Book of Days* contains quirky, eccentric, amusing and important events and facts from different periods of history, many of which had a major impact on the religious and political history of Britain as a whole. Ideal for dipping into, this addictive little book will keep you entertained and informed. Featuring hundreds of snippets of information gleaned from the vaults of Oxford's archives, it delights residents and visitors alike.

978-0-7524-6550-0

The Aston Martin Story
JOHN CHRISTOPHER

This is a fresh look at 100 years of Britain's most iconic car company, Aston Martin, from the origins of the Aston Martin marque, through the gadget-laden stars of numerous James Bond films, to the prestigious super-cars that continue to be market leaders throughout the world. This book tells the whole story of the classic motor manufacturer, covering how it got its name to its latest models, and everything in between.

978-0-7524-7133-4

Visit our website and discover thousands of other History Press books.

www.thehistorypress.co.uk